Why Life Hurts

Understanding Why God Allows Pain, Suffering, and Evil

Jim Scudder

Victory In Grace
60 Quentin Road
Lake Zurich, IL 60047
1-800-78-GRACE
www.victoryingrace.org

Printed in the USA
Signature Book Printing, www.sbpbooks.com

Dedication

This book is dedicated to my delightful wife, Karen. She is my helper, friend, confidant, and partner for life.

Acknowledgements

I also want to express my appreciation for the many people who helped this book become a reality. Jason Tanney and Cameron Edwards were my editors; Lydia McConnell, David Kumura, Allan Hudson, Andrew Collison, and Barb Vanden Bosch proofed the project; Dan Reehoff assisted with the cover design; and Kari Kumura arranged the text for the book's layout and designed the cover.

Table of Contents

Foreword

One of the great questions of life is, why do God's children have to suffer? In the book, *Why Life Hurts*, my son, Jim, has written masterfully on that important question in a short, precise, easy-to-understand manner. Because the ups and downs of our lives have much more significance than we can grasp ourselves, understanding arises by seeking answers in the Word of God. When we seek the Lord's response to our heartfelt questions, we learn the answer to those questions.

Sometimes when discouragement comes, you wonder if it is all really worth it: Why should I go on? What's the meaning of life? Why do others seem to do better than I do? I try so hard, yet God seems to forget who I am.

Answers to these questions and many more will assure and comfort you as you read this book.

Not only should you read this book, but I recommend you tell your friends about it and have them read it, too. It will do them a world of good.

Dr. James A. Scudder, Sr.

Introduction

There are two types of people—those who are currently suffering a tragedy and those who will soon be suffering a tragedy. I'm sorry if this sounds fatalistic. It's simply reality.

The purpose of this book is to help those of us who are perplexed by the frequent and systematic occurrence of calamity. "Why" is the first question that pops into our heads. Why is there pain? Why is there suffering? Why is there evil?

Many years ago, a terrible famine slowly put its stranglehold on Russia. A peasant described it like this: "We've eaten everything we could lay our hands on—cats, dogs, field mice, birds. When it's light tomorrow, you will see the trees stripped of their bark."

Why?

Why is there famine?

Why would God allow such suffering?

It is estimated that one-third of the world is underfed and one-third is starving. Millions of people die of starvation each year, and a large percentage of children under six years old are undernourished.

As a father of two, the thought of children starving breaks my heart. I could give example after example of tragedy after tragedy—and many find themselves forced to ask the question, If God is good, how can He allow suffering and evil to go on seemingly without restraint?

This question will be asked until the very end of time. It is natural for us to question someone's love if the person does not seem to care. But at the same time, we must be very careful about jumping to conclusions.

Two people I have recently had the privilege of meeting have provided inspiration for this book. One is Marjorie, and the other is Lior.

Marjorie has cancer. While speaking at my sister's church in Chili, Ohio, I was asked to visit her. She had already outlived the predicted time the doctors had given her. Marjorie asked me, "Why?" Not "Why do I have cancer?" but "Why has God given me 'bonus' days?" I told her that perhaps it was because she had more to do.

She flashed a big smile and said some words I will never forget—"The big 'C' in me is not cancer. It's…"—well, that will have to wait until the end of the book.

Lior is the other person who gave me reasons to write about this topic. He sat next to me on a flight from India to Israel. I struck up a conversation with him, and learned he was an Israeli dentist. We had a great time talking about all sorts of things (except pulling teeth!), and the conversation turned to proofs that God exists. I told Lior that he was proof of God's existence.

He looked at me funny and asked, "Why?"

I said because God had preserved the Jews through centuries of abuse, torture, and threatened extermination, and had returned them to their homeland as promised (Ezekiel 37).

He said, "That's why I don't believe in God."

I asked, "Why?"

He said, "Because God, as described in the Scriptures, could not possibly allow six million Jews to be massacred in the Holocaust."

My dentist friend's sentiment is echoed by many today as mankind tries to understand how a good God can allow suffering and evil.

To answer a question much bigger than my small brain can handle, I suggest we turn to what **God** has said about these things.

That is what this book is about—attempting to give you, Marjorie, and Lior answers to questions about the character of God. Reading what God said will be important to getting answers, but the real proof of His character is what He has done. That will truly paint a picture of what

He is like. Then we will finally be able to understand life's **big picture** and answer that burning question, Why does God allow pain, suffering, and evil?

CHAPTER 1

The Big Picture

As I contemplate heartbreak and suffering, I immediately think of a man named Job.

Job was a very wealthy man. He lived in the lap of luxury. As one author put it, "He was Howard Hughes, John D. Rockefeller, and Henry Ford all rolled into one." He had 7,000 sheep, 3,000 camels, 500 yoke of oxen, and 500 donkeys. The Bible says, *this man was the greatest of all the men of the east.* Job 1:3

We are also told he was *perfect and upright, and one that feared God, and eschewed* [shunned] *evil.* Job 1:1 What does it mean when it says Job was perfect? Did he finally figure out how to never sin? He never lied, stole, coveted, or lusted? Did he never say anything hurtful—words he wished he could take back? No. But it does mean he was perfect in his relationship to God.

Job understood that he was a sinner. He was no different from you or me. The book of Romans tells us that all have sinned. Job knew because of sins he had already committed that even if he never sinned again, payment for those past sins must be made. He knew he could not pay the price himself. He neither trusted himself, nor his works, to make himself right before God; therefore, we see that his total faith was in God. He believed that God would one day provide a perfect sacrifice for him. That made him perfect in the eyes of God.

Even though works do not save, God wanted Job to offer burnt sacrifices. This was a work. Although this neither saved him, nor kept him saved, it helped him and his family understand the cost of sin. Innocent blood had to be shed. The sacrifices showed the world that his faith and trust was in the One True God.

Job loved and feared God, so he sacrificed to Him, and therefore was in a right relationship with Him.

Job not only had a lot of material things and a right relationship with God, but he also had many children — ten in fact, seven sons and three daughters. And since he was wealthy, his kids lived in luxury and ease. It was a fairytale life … **until one awful day**.

It started like any other day—plenty to eat, plenty to drink, a nice day in a nice life. But then Job's breathless servants began running up to him with very bad news.

"The oxen and donkeys have been stolen and the servants killed!" said one.

"Fire from Heaven burned up the sheep and killed more servants!" cried another.

"Master, your camels have been taken and more servants slain!" moaned another.

At this point, Job himself must have had a hard time breathing. But worse was yet to come. As he was receiving the news of the loss of all his possessions, something far more precious than possessions was also taken from him — his children. Another servant said that a terrible wind caused the house to collapse and all inside were killed.

Now Job collapsed. Surely he would cry out and ask God why. He would say **it's not fair!** Surely he would blame God for bringing great pain and anguish into his life.

But wait … he did fall on the ground — not to blame God, but to praise Him!

He then uttered these famous words, *Naked came I out of my mother's womb, and naked shall I return thither: the LORD gave, and the LORD hath taken away; blessed be the name of the LORD.* Job 1:21

You see, what Job did not know was that Satan was in Heaven accusing him of only praising God when things were good. But God knew Job better than the Devil. God did allow the Wicked One to bring tragedy and loss upon Job. But don't ever blame God for evil. It was Satan, not God, who did these things.

This verse says it well: *Let no man say when he is tempted, I am tempted of God: for God cannot be tempted with evil, neither tempteth he any man.* James 1:13

15

Let me be clear — if anyone or anything was to blame for Job's calamities, it was Satan and sin. God is good. Job was correct in giving Him praise, not blame.

There is a principle that we will explore later in this book — God can take what Satan and sin intend for evil and turn the situation into good. In Job's case, God allowed these bad things to fall upon him so that Job would show the old Devil that his love for God was not because of the things he had been given, but because he simply loved and feared God for Who He was.

God held the Devil within certain parameters. Initially, he could not touch Job himself. I think that shows God's goodness. Another thing that shows God's goodness was that God gave Job twice as much as he had before.

This story illustrates two things to me:
1. God is not the author of evil.
2. We can't always see the big picture.

Job had no idea of what had gone on between God and Satan.

Job did not know that this was a test allowed by the God Who loved him.

Many times we might never be able to get all the facts. There are things that might have happened behind the scenes that you will not know or understand until much later.

I remember visiting a rug factory in Egypt. It was a place where they made silk carpets the old-fashioned way. As I walked in, the first thing I saw made me almost laugh. The rug that was being worked on in front of me was terrible. I would never in a million years buy such a hideous thing. I could not imagine even taking it as a gift. I would certainly NEVER put that ugly thing in my house! Then I walked around to the other side. My jaw dropped. It was the most beautiful, exquisite piece of art I had ever seen. If only I had enough money to buy it…. I would have proudly put it in the most prominent place in my home, showing all my guests this incredible masterpiece!

What changed? My view. When I walked in, I was looking at the back. It was not a nice thing to see. It was filled with irregularities and chaos. That's just like life — many things just don't make sense. We ask, "Why." Maybe we should change the question to what — What do You want me to learn from this, dear God?

One day, it will all make perfect sense. One day, you will see the big picture. Until then, do as Job did. Praise God, for He is so good!

He wants the best for us. He wants to make a masterpiece out of you and me. Let Him. He cares about the smallest things — even the sparrows (Luke 12:6–7).

How much more must He love us who are made in His image!

CHAPTER 2

The Blame Game

The question we must begin with is not, why does God allow evil? but, where did evil come from?

According to Genesis, the book of beginnings, God created the heavens and the Earth, and all things that dwell on the Earth. This beautiful, blue orb, with all its wonders and splendor, was spoken into existence. And God said it was good.

Our great-great-great-great- (you get the picture) grand-parents lived in a garden called Eden. Picture rivers and streams, waterfalls, colorful birds, and great beasts as gentle as lambs. There was plenty to eat, drink, and do. It was paradise — no pain, or disease, or death ... **or evil**.

God put a particular tree in the middle of all the trees in the garden. Without this tree, called "The Tree of the Knowledge of Good and Evil," humans would be no more than robots. True love is only true if you choose to love and are not forced. God did not want to force us to love Him, or it would not be love. So by giving Adam and Eve a choice, He was willing to allow us to make the wrong choice. It's called free will, and we all have it.

Well, wouldn't you know it—we made the wrong choice. And I don't think it took too long.

Lucifer, God's highest created angel, decided he wanted to be in charge. Pride got the best of him, and he took a third of the angels with him. Now, we find him here on the scene of the first human sin.

In the form of a serpent, he tricks Eve. He uses her senses of hearing, sight, touch, and taste to tempt her to do what she knows God said not to do. (And what's amazing to me is Eve and Adam had thousands of trees to eat from and only one they could not! God is not in the business of trying to tempt us to sin just so He can zap us. It is quite the opposite.)

Eve eats of the fruit, then Adam—and so began the first of thousands of years of suffering. Sin was passed down from father to child, from generation to generation. Sin presently reigns supreme in this world, and can be traced back to this moment in the garden.

So if we are looking for someone to blame, we must first look at ourselves. And <u>Satan should not be far behind in the blame game.</u>

There were many consequences for sin: pain in childbirth, thorns, thistles, and weeds. Earning a living was made very difficult. But the worst result of sin was death.

At the very moment of the first sin, Adam and Eve died spiritually, and they began to die physically. This is proved by the fact that their innocence was gone, and they realized their nakedness. They put together leaves to clothe themselves and hid from God.

The best part of the perfect creation was the perfect fellowship between the Creator and man. That was now in shambles. But God, in His great and wonderful love, took the first step to remedy the problem man created. He made the first sacrifice by shedding the blood of an animal and clothing Adam and Eve with the skins. This would have been the first time they saw an animal die. And it was because of them.

To understand why there is evil, we must comprehend the holiness of God. He is perfect, righteous, and holy. He can't even **look** at sin. Sin is missing the mark of His perfection. One sin separates us from Him, and the Bible says we have all fallen short of the glory of God (Romans 3:23).

We were created to have fellowship with the Creator, so something had to be done to restore that fellowship. God had a plan. In fact, the plan was in place before the creation of the world (1 Peter 1:20). Mankind must be—and would be—redeemed!

CHAPTER 3

The Undisputed Love of God

If God is not the author of evil, and Satan and mankind are to blame for sin, then how should we feel about the God Who got all this going in the first place?

I certainly don't understand why so many terrible things happen. Why did my Grandmother Esther die from cancer? Why does my father have diabetes and heart trouble? Why do I have asthma and back pain? Why do earthquakes happen like the one in Haiti, killing hundreds of thousands of people? Why are there tsunamis that wipe whole towns away like in Japan? Why did the United States get attacked on September 11th, 2001? Truly, these things are beyond my finite ability to understand.

But I have learned at least one thing in my life—**I must not dare question the love of Someone Who made the ultimate sacrifice for me!**

Let me explain. The Creator God could have said,

Those humans! They can't stay out of trouble. I made them and their environment perfect, and now look what they have done. I will give them what they deserve. Let them lie, cheat, covet, and kill—I don't care. Let them pay for their own sin. Let them spend eternity in the place I made for the devil and the demons. Their destination is a place of darkness, separation, and fire, but their bad choices are not My problem.

The above paragraph could be true, but praise God it's not. Although God is holy, righteous, and just, He is also love. Yes, our disobedience **must** be punished, or He would not be God; yet He made a way for us to escape Hellfire. This is why I say God's love should never be questioned—because He sent His only Son to take our place.

Let me refer back to my children for a moment. Let's assume I would allow one of my daughters to die in the place of a murderer/rapist who is next on death row. Many would correctly question my sanity, but the inmate would never question what I just demonstrated—love for a sinner.

That's why I love the following verses so much: *For scarcely for a righteous man will one die: yet peradventure* [perhaps] *for a good man some would even dare to die. But God commendeth* [demonstrated] *his love toward us, in that, while we were yet sinners, Christ died for us.* Romans 5:7–8 In other words, rarely does someone die in the place of a good person, let alone for one who is guilty.

Now you might be saying about now, I'm not that bad. I'm surely better than most! The question is not, are we better than most? but, are we completely free of sin? The Bible says no. *For all have sinned, and come short of the glory of God.* Romans 3:23

People ask me, "Why do bad things happen to good people?" My response, although Biblical, is not often kindly accepted. "First of all, there really are no such things as **good** people — we **all** have fallen short of God's perfection."

Think of it this way — if Heaven is perfect, how could a perfect and holy God allow even one sin into a perfect place? Heaven would no longer be perfect.

That is why the Son of God left His glory in Heaven and came to this fallen Earth. He became a man (while fully God), lived a perfect life of 33 years, and yet was nailed to a cross as a sinner, even though He had not sinned. Wow! What amazing love!

For God so loved the world, that he gave his only begotten Son, that whosoever believeth in him should not perish, but have everlasting life. John 3:16

Greater love hath no man than this, that a man lay down his life for his friends. John 15:13

This is why I have come to the wise conclusion never to question God's love!

CHAPTER 4

The Gift of Pain

Now that we know God is not the author of evil and that He has made the ultimate sacrifice proving His love, some ask the question, "Why did He create pain?"

When I think of trying to understand the **point of pain**, I think of one man, Dr. Paul W. Brand. He was a gifted orthopedic surgeon who ministered in India alongside a relative of mine, Dr. Ida Scudder. She started the Christian Medical College and Hospital in Vellore, India, and Dr. Brand and his wife began teaching there in 1946.

It was there that the Brands first came across victims of leprosy. These deformed and crippled people agonized alone because others were fearful of contracting this terrible disease. Deeply affected by these poor souls, he and his wife dedicated themselves to relieving their suffering.

He soon discovered that those with leprosy were losing their hands and feet, not from the disease itself, but from the disease destroying their nerves. He found that leprosy attacks mainly the nervous system. The resultant tissue damage occurs because the patient loses the warnings of pain—not because of inherent decay brought on by the disease. Dr. Brand discovered **the gift of pain**.

It is unusual to think of pain this way. It does not seem right that pain-deprived people inadvertently injure and destroy themselves. But it is a truth.

After reading about Dr. Brand and his research, I have not thought of pain in the same way. I still don't relish the thought of getting an injury or hurting myself, but now I know that pain can be looked at as good and truly as a gift from God.

Someone has written the following list based on Dr. Brand's study, and I could not say it better myself:

10 Reasons to Believe in a God Who Allows Suffering:

1. Suffering comes with the freedom to choose.
"Would we take freedom from the possibility of pain in exchange for the loss of free will?" (Dr. Paul Brand)

2. Suffering reveals what is in our own hearts.
"Times of pain bring fear, which strips the mental and physical mask." (Dr. Paul Brand)

3. Suffering takes us to the edge of eternity.
Blessed are the poor in spirit: for theirs is the kingdom of heaven. Blessed are they that mourn: for they shall be comforted. Blessed are the meek: for they shall inherit the earth. Matthew 5:3–5

4. God can turn suffering around for our good.
Joseph's story — God meant for good what his brothers meant for evil. (Genesis 37–50)

5. Pain can warn us of danger.
Leprosy—Loss of pain sensation causes damage.

6. In times of crisis, we find one another.
People help each other in natural disasters and accidents.

7. Suffering gives the opportunity to trust God.
Instead of asking, "Why me?" we should ask, "What now, Lord?"

8. Pain loosens our grip on life.
In my Father's house are many mansions: if it were not so, I would have told you. I go to prepare a place for you. And if I go and prepare a place for you, I will come again, and receive you unto myself; that where I am, there ye may be also. John 14:2–3

9. God suffers with us in our sufferings.
He is despised and rejected of men; a man of sorrows, and acquainted with grief: and we hid as it were our faces from him; he was despised, and we esteemed him not. Surely he hath borne our griefs, and carried our sorrows: yet we did esteem him stricken, smitten of God, and afflicted. But he was wounded for our transgressions, he was bruised for our iniquities: the chastisement of our peace was upon him; and with his stripes we are healed. Isaiah 53:3–5

10. God's comfort is greater than our suffering.
And he said unto me, My grace is sufficient for thee: for my strength is made perfect in weakness. Most gladly therefore will I rather glory in my infirmities, that the power of Christ may rest upon me. Therefore

I take pleasure in infirmities, in reproaches, in necessities, in persecutions, in distresses for Christ's sake: for when I am weak, then am I strong. 2 Corinthians 12:9–10

As we look at pain now as a gift, let's look at two people who have accepted and used this gift:

1. The great musician and composer, George Frideric Handel, suffered a stroke and temporarily lost the use of his right arm. Just a few years later, deep in debt and despair, he had the inspiration to write *The Messiah.*

2. Helen Keller, blind and deaf, has written, "I thank God for my handicaps, for through them I have found myself, my work, and God."

These examples of people who suffered from pain and physical problems were not hindered by pain, but helped.

May we finally realize that pain can be, and is, a gift.

CHAPTER 5

The Messy Molding Method

Pigs are messy. Someone once said, "Some people are like pigs. They can never look up until laid on their backs!"

Although this quote may seem strange, if you would examine a pig's eyes, you'll find that this is true. Their eyes are designed to look down.

Many are like pigs (no offense!). So often we are victims of an earthward, downward gaze. But God, in His goodness, allows affliction by putting us on our backs that we might look up to Him.

Just as pigs are messy, so is **molding**. Just as pigs usually wallow around in the mud, so God can take that mud and make a masterpiece.

When an artisan takes a lump of clay, only he has a picture in his mind of what that silly, little lump can become.

He takes the clay and starts pounding it back and forth in his hands. Wham! Wham! Wham! I know the lump of clay is thinking, Ouch! Ouch! Ouch!

Then the master craftsman rubs the lump into a round ball. The clay thinks, This is more like it!

Suddenly, the maker hits the lump with all his force and continues to push, knocking the breath out of the poor lump. This lasts until the lump is ready to go on the potter's wheel.

Now the lump thinks, I have gone through all this pain and anguish, and now he wants to make me seasick! What's the point of all this, anyway? I liked being just a lump! Yes, it was a little boring, but is all this suffering worth it?

Around and around the lump goes on the wheel. Slowly, slowly, the craftsman forms the clay. Little by little, the lump is transformed.

Finally, it seems like the master knows what he is doing. The lump likes what is happening until suddenly, the master sighs and firmly smashes the clay back into a ball.

The lump of clay is sooooo discouraged. At this point, it is thinking, What now? This man is a maniac! Surely he does not know what he is doing, nor does he really care about me. He is just having fun at my expense.

But the man is not done. He had seen something the lump could not—a small defect that would have shelved him for the rest of his life if the master had continued without starting over.

Slowly, slowly, he begins again. This time, a real work of art is coming almost magically out of his gentle hands.

Finally, after much pounding, prodding, stretching, and molding, he is done. What a work of beauty and grace he has made — and none of it would have been possible if the clay had not been willing to suffer!

This lump of clay is now a vessel worthy of sitting on the finest of tables and serving the highest of royalty.

I guess I really don't need to comment further. We have looked at pigs and at clay. I'm sure you get the idea, but let's also take a look at diamonds.

What can diamonds teach us? Diamonds are made from carbon under intense pressure. Then they are mined, cut to shape, and polished.

Like the intense pressure which transforms what appears to be a worthless piece of carbon into diamonds, God takes bad and somehow does good with it. This is a Biblical principle that we will fully explore next.

Let me end this chapter with this. Consider the value of steel:
- A bar of steel is worth $5.
- If made into horseshoes, it is worth $10.
- If made into needles, it is worth $350.
- If made into penknife blades, it is worth $32,000.
- And if it is made into springs for watches, it is worth $250,000!

What a drilling the poor bar must undergo to be worth a greater value. But the more it is manipulated, the more it is hammered and passed through the fire, the more it is beaten and pounded and polished, the greater its value.

Those who suffer most are capable of yielding most; and it is through the messy process of pain and suffering that God can get the most out of us.

CHAPTER 6

The Soft Pillow for a Tired Heart

The late R. A. Torrey had an unusual name for a well-known verse of the Bible. He called Romans 8:28 "a soft pillow for a tired heart."

And we know that all things work together for good to them that love God, to them who are the called according to his purpose. Romans 8:28

Many Christians have lain their heads on this promise. It is a balm for the broken and a salve for the suffering.

The phrase "we know" is often missed when we read this. If you are like me, you want to skip right to the good stuff! But these two seemingly insignificant words are the good stuff.

This is a phrase that indicates most Christians know this is a truth by experience. And if you have not yet experienced this truth, you will.

God, in His infinite wisdom and sovereignty, has not only the ability, but also the knowledge to make bad things that He did not cause, but did allow, to bring about something great—and it's greater than if the bad thing had not happened at all. He does all of this without conflicting with man's free will.

This principle should be a part of a dedicated Christian's regular experience. It is something "we know." Does anyone have to tell you that honey is sweet? Does anyone have to tell you that God is good? No. As the sweetness of honey is proven by tasting it, so the goodness of God is proven by experiencing it over and over. Yes, He is good; but not just good—VERY GOOD!

Radio teacher, J. Vernon McGee, said, *"All things—good and bad; bright and dark; sweet and bitter; easy and hard; happy and sad; prosperity and poverty; health and sickness; calm and storm; comfort and suffering; life and death."*

This verse also points out that working out all things for good is done for those who "love God." Love is essential. He loves us. His love should inspire love in return.

John the Apostle explains this: *Herein is love, not that we loved God, but that he loved us, and sent his Son to be the propitiation* [seat of mercy] *for our sins. Beloved, if God so loved us, we ought also to love one another. … And we have known and believed the love that God hath to us. God is love; and he that dwelleth in love dwelleth in God, and God in him.* 1 John 4:10–11, 16

To handle pain and suffering, we simply need to love God and trust that He wants the best for us.

John also says, *We love him, because he first loved us.* 1 John 4:19 What will bring about brightness to your daily outlook is an honest love for God.

I really believe one day we will be able to echo Job's words, *Though he slay me, yet will I trust in him....* Job 13:15

As we look with amazement at the beautiful tapestry of our lives, we will share Joseph's sentiments, *God meant it unto good....* Genesis 50:20

Resting our tired heads on the pillow of Romans 8:28 will give us a whole new outlook on life.

It will be like the woman who viewed the scene of a horrific earthquake with a smile. When asked how she could smile in the wake of such destruction, she replied, "I rejoice that I have a God Who can shake the world!"

She was not happy about losing her home, but she could still rejoice in God's power because she could rest her head on the pillow of God's caring love.

CHAPTER 7

The Day Suffering Goes Away

When Benjamin Franklin was about to die, he asked that a picture of Christ on the cross should be placed in his bedroom so that he could look, as he said, "upon the form of the Silent Sufferer."

Benjamin Franklin wrote in advance the epitaph that would be on his gravestone: "The body of Benjamin Franklin, Printer, like the cover of an old book, its contents torn out and stripped of its lettering and gilding, lies here. ... Yet the work itself shall not be lost; for it will, as he believed, appear once more in a new and more beautiful edition, corrected and amended by the Author."

Both physical and emotional pain seems to follow us through life. It is as if we are torn and stripped. But like old Ben, we must remember that it will be worth it all when we see Jesus.

He will bear the only physical deformity in Heaven. I believe that just as He showed His nail-scarred hands and feet and spear-scarred side to the disciples, so we will also be able to see and feel His scars. This will help us eternally remember the suffering He endured for each of us.

Adoniram Judson, the renowned missionary to Burma, endured untold hardships trying to reach the lost for Christ. For seven heartbreaking years, he suffered hunger and adversity. During this time, he was thrown into Ava Prison, and for seventeen months was subjected to almost unbelievable mistreatment. As a result, he carried the ugly marks made by the chains and iron shackles which had cruelly bound him for the rest of his life. Undaunted, upon his release he asked for permission to enter another province where he might resume preaching the gospel. The godless ruler indignantly denied his request, saying, "My people are not fools enough to listen to anything a missionary might **say**, but I fear they might be impressed by your **scars** and turn to your religion!"

Although I don't believe we will carry physical scars to Heaven like Christ, may we remember that if we suffer here for Him, we will be rewarded in Glory.

I'm sure Adoniram thought of Heaven when we was suffering for the Lord. That is what motivated him to continue on to the very end!

Think of these verses:

And there shall be no more curse: but the throne of God and of the Lamb shall be in it; and his servants shall serve him: And they shall see his face; and his name shall be in their foreheads. And there shall be no night there; and they need no candle, neither light of the sun; for the Lord God giveth them light: and they shall reign for ever and ever. Revelation 22:3–5

The next time you are suffering, think of the day when there will be no more pain, disease, or evil. Oh, what a day that will be!

CHAPTER 8

The Choice Is Yours

The preacher, Charles Spurgeon, tells this story:

There was a certain king whose son was sent on an errand to a far country, and when he came into that country, although he was the lawful prince of it, he found that the citizens would not acknowledge him. They mocked at him, jeered at him, and took him and set him in stocks. There they scoffed at him and pelted him with filth.

Now there was one in that country who knew the prince, and he alone stood up for him when all the mob was raging against him. This man stood side-by-side to wipe the filth from that dear, royal face; and when from cruel hands objects were thrown, this man took his full share; and whenever he could, he thrust himself before the prince to ward off the blows from him if possible, and to bear the scorn instead of him.

Now it came to pass that after awhile, the prince went on his way, and in time the man who had been the prince's friend was called to the king's palace. And on a day when all the princes of the court were around, and the peers and nobles of the land were sitting in their places, the king came to his throne and he called for that man, and he said, "Make way, princes and nobles! Make way! Here is a man more noble than you all, for he stood boldly forth with my son when he was scorned and scoffed at! Make way, I say, each one of you, for he shall sit at my right hand with my own son. As he took a share of his scorn, he shall now take a share of his honor.

And there sat princes and nobles who wished that they had been there—they now envied the man who had been privileged to endure scorn and scoffing for the prince's sake!

I like this story because it helps believers to remember that it is an honor to suffer for our Savior! But what if you are reading this and Jesus is not your Savior? What if suffering has made you angry at God?

Perhaps this book has shown you that God does indeed love you... that God is not the author of evil ... that even pain and suffering can **help** you if you are willing to trust Him.

The choice is yours. Are you trusting Him? Have you trusted Him? By that, I mean have you ever made a decision to accept His free gift of everlasting life? Do you realize as a sinner you need a Savior? Will you right now place your total trust in the only One willing and able to save you?

Eternal life cannot be earned. If it could, Jesus would not have had to suffer and die. But He did suffer and die—and He is alive today.

He is saying, *Come. And let him that heareth say, Come. And let him that is athirst come. And whosoever will, let him take the water of life freely.* Revelation 22:17

These verses say it so well: *For by grace are ye saved through faith; and that not of yourselves: it is the gift of God: Not of works, lest any man should boast.* Ephesians 2:8–9

God does love you! He sent His Son to die for you! He suffered your Hell for you! I beg you—trust in Him now.

Pain, suffering, and evil do exist now, but don't blame God. He is love. That has been proven beyond any doubt. And one day, evil will be completely eradicated. Until that day, love and serve God with all your heart, soul, strength, and mind.

Do you remember Marjorie from the introduction? She had lived past the six months the doctors had told her to expect. Now she knew that every day she was alive was a special gift from God. She knew that to waste even a minute of a day complaining of her plight would be to squander an opportunity to serve God that she could never get back. She knew and lived these truths because she had accepted God's gift of eternal life and was living a "thank-you-letter life" (maybe another book!).

As we were leaving, the last thing Marjorie told me was, "The big 'C' in me is not cancer—it's Christ."

Is the big "C" in you Christ? It can be today!

If you would like to learn how to make sure Christ
is the big "C" in your life, or if you would like more
information about *Victory In Grace*, please call
1-800-78-GRACE, or visit the "Salvation" page on
our website, www.victoryingrace.org.